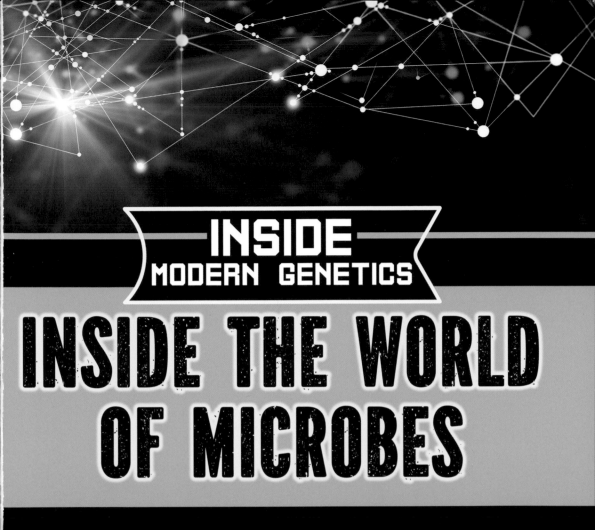

INSIDE
MODERN GENETICS

INSIDE THE WORLD OF MICROBES

HOWARD PHILLIPS

ROSEN
PUBLISHING

NEW YORK

Published in 2022 by The Rosen Publishing Group, Inc.
29 East 21st Street, New York, NY 10010

First Edition

Designer: Rachel Rising
Editor: Greg Roza

Portions of this work were originally authored by Janey Levy and published as *The World of Microbes, Bacteria, Viruses, and Other Microorganisms*. All new material in this edition was authored by Howard Phillips.

Library of Congress Cataloging-in-Publication Data

Names: Phillips, Howard, 1971- author.
Title: Inside the world of microbes / Howard Phillips.
Description: New York : Rosen Publishing, [2022] | Series: Inside modern genetics | Includes index.
Identifiers: LCCN 2021033499 (print) | LCCN 2021033500 (ebook) | ISBN 9781499470505 (library binding) | ISBN 9781499470499 (paperback) | ISBN 9781499470512 (ebook)
Subjects: LCSH: Microorganisms--Juvenile literature. | Bacteria--Juvenile literature. | Viruses--Juvenile literature.
Classification: LCC QR57 .P45 2022 (print) | LCC QR57 (ebook) | DDC 579--dc23
LC record available at https://lccn.loc.gov/2021033499
LC ebook record available at https://lccn.loc.gov/2021033500

Some of the images in this book illustrate individuals who are models. The depictions do not imply actual situations or events.

Manufactured in the United States of America

CPSIA Compliance Information: Batch #CWRYA22. For further information contact Rosen Publishing, New York, New York at 1-800-237-9932.

CONTENTS

INTRODUCTION

To many people, the words "bacteria" and "virus" result in worry and fear. Much of this concern is caused by the news. Reporters recount alarming tales of flesh-eating bacteria and of people who died from food contaminated with the bacterium *Escherichia coli* (better known simply as *E. coli*). They announce fears of epidemics of viral diseases such as bird flu and swine flu. Our world changed dramatically during the COVID-19 pandemic, caused by a new strain of coronavirus. The stories can make people feel as if these microbes are out to get humans. In fact, as a group, microbes are more beneficial to us than they are harmful. Knowing more about them improves understanding of the good they do and the bounty of knowledge they offer us regarding life processes and genetics.

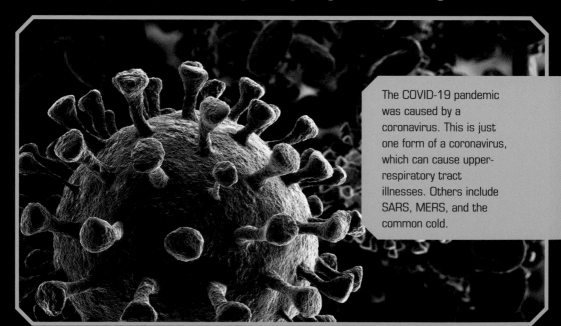

The COVID-19 pandemic was caused by a coronavirus. This is just one form of a coronavirus, which can cause upper-respiratory tract illnesses. Others include SARS, MERS, and the common cold.

A microbe is a unicellular (single-celled) organism so small it can't be seen without a microscope. Bacteria, archaea (once considered "strange" bacteria), and most protists (including the organisms commonly known as protozoans and some algae) are microbes. Viruses, which aren't cells, are even smaller microbes. Microbes are everywhere! They're on Earth's surface and in the soil. Some live deep underground. Famed naturalist E. O. Wilson gave a speech (which can be read in Tim Friend's book *The Third Domain*) in which he said the mass of microbes living underground may be greater than the combined mass of all living organisms on Earth's surface. Many microbes live in Earth's oceans and in some of the planet's harshest environments, including deep sea hot water vents.

Microbes live in colorful swaths along the rim of a hot water geyser in Yellowstone National Park.

What causes many people to worry is that millions upon millions of microbes live on and inside people. Microbiologist Dorothy Crawford reports in *Deadly Companions* that one person may be home to 100 trillion microbes. Crawford and Friend both note that this equals about 10 microbes for each cell in the human body. Crawford calls microbes "deadly companions." While it's true that some microbes can sicken and kill people, it's hardly true that they all do. Many are helpful, and many are even essential to human existence. Physician and writer Jeanette Farrell calls microbes "invisible allies" in her book of the same name.

Geneticists studying microbes have revealed much about the origin of life on Earth and the life processes that continue to keep organisms alive. Scientists continue to study microbes of many kinds with the aim of understanding more about all life on Earth, including human life. This is possible, in part, because of a phenomenon called the conservation of genes across species. This simply means that the gene responsible for a specific task in one species will be very much like the gene responsible for that task in other species. This allows biologists to take what they learn about genes in microbes and apply it to other organisms. Scientists don't have to use microbes for this research; they could use genes from any species. However, microbes can be grown quickly and cheaply in the laboratory, can be stored almost indefinitely, and are easy to work with.

Geneticists still study microbes in the hope of learning more about all life on Earth.

CHAPTER 1

UNDERSTANDING GENETICS

Genetics is the branch of biology that studies heredity and variation in organisms. All fields of study, including genetics, have their own words, and anyone who wants to understand genetics must know at least a few key terms. An obvious place to start is the term "gene." Genes are the basic units of heredity. These tiny molecules are the elements in each cell that determine what traits an organism inherits from its parents. This is true of all creatures—from a tiny fruit fly to a human being.

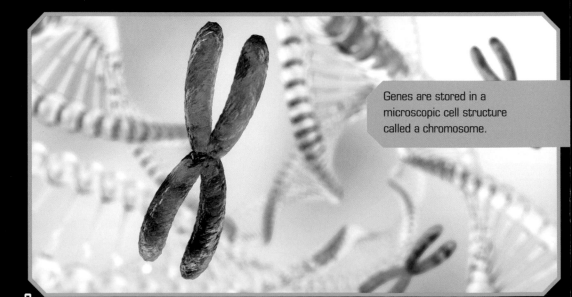

Genes are stored in a microscopic cell structure called a chromosome.

Chromosomes are the cell structures where genes are located. Chromosomes are made of protein molecules and a substance called deoxyribonucleic acid, or DNA. An organism's complete set of DNA is called its genome. However, a genome contains more than genes. DNA segments contain information that is "non-coding," which means it's unrelated to heredity. Scientists once called these genes "junk genes" because they thought they had no purpose. Individual genes are DNA segments that contain the "code" necessary to making the proteins that support life. For these instructions to be carried out, DNA needs help. This help comes from another substance called ribonucleic acid, or RNA. RNA takes DNA's instructions and helps the cell execute them. In some viruses, RNA replaces DNA as a carrier of genetic codes.

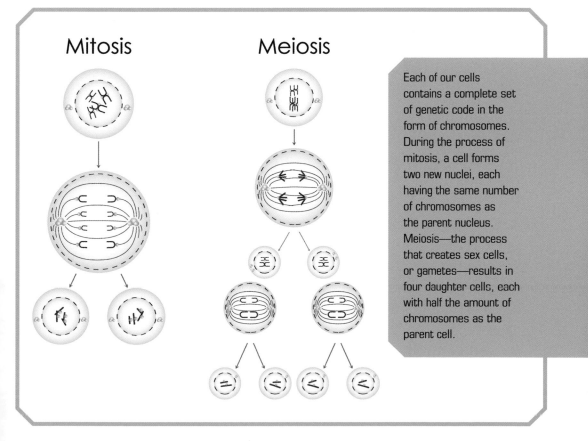

Mitosis

Meiosis

Each of our cells contains a complete set of genetic code in the form of chromosomes. During the process of mitosis, a cell forms two new nuclei, each having the same number of chromosomes as the parent nucleus. Meiosis—the process that creates sex cells, or gametes—results in four daughter cells, each with half the amount of chromosomes as the parent cell.

THE HISTORY OF GENETICS

In the 1850s, Austrian botanist Gregor Mendel conducted experiments on the heredity of traits in pea plants. As an Augustinian monk, Mendel carried out all his experiments at St. Thomas's Abbey in Brno, now in the Czech Republic. His studies led him to work out the basic rules governing how information is passed from one generation to the next.

Mendel published his work in 1866. However, Mendel's findings went largely unnoticed until 1900, when they were rediscovered by botanists Carl Erich Correns, Erich Tschermak von Seysenegg, and Hugo de Vries. That was shortly after the discovery of chromosomes, which was made possible thanks to more powerful microscopes. Although the compound microscope was invented around 1590, it wasn't until the 1800s, when better glass-making methods yielded improved microscopes, that scientists could see inside cells and discover chromosomes.

Studies of cells and cell reproduction convinced some scientists that chromosomes formed the foundation of heredity, although no experimental evidence existed. Proof soon came from new experiments. Beginning in 1909, biologist Thomas Hunt Morgan led a team of scientists investigating the inheritance of traits over several generations. The scientists used fruit flies because they grow and reproduce rapidly and possess numerous traits that can be easily tracked over generations. Their research proved that genes are the units of heredity and they're located on chromosomes. Morgan and his team also produced the first genetic map. Genetic changes, called mutations, are easily observed in fruit flies. These mutations helped Morgan's team determine each gene's location and the trait it affected.

In the 1940s, biologist George W. Beadle and biochemist Edward L. Tatum conducted experiments on a mold (a kind of fungus) and showed how genes direct the production of special

Morgan and his team used flies of the *Drosophila* genus. This tiny organism has continued to be used in genetic experiments to this day.

proteins called enzymes. The enzymes in turn control chemical reactions in cells. Beadle and Tatum also demonstrated that each gene controls the production of one specific enzyme. However, an important question still remained: Which material in chromosomes made up the genes?

DEOXYRIBONUCLEIC ACID

Scientists had long known that chromosomes contain proteins and DNA. However, DNA (isolated by biologist Johann Friedrich Miescher in 1869) was largely ignored. The processes of life require proteins, and most scientists believed chromosomal proteins determined heredity. That view prevailed until 1944, when physician Oswald T. Avery and a team of scientists demonstrated that DNA decides heredity in bacteria.

DNA is composed of chemical building blocks called nucleotides. Nucleotides contain three components: a phosphate group, a sugar (deoxyribose), and a base. Nucleotides are all identical except for their bases, which is why scientists identify them by their base. The four DNA bases are adenine (A), guanine (G), thymine (T), and cytosine (C).

In 1953, biologists James Watson and Francis Crick proposed that the shape of DNA resembles a ladder twisted into a spiral, a shape called a double helix. The phosphate and sugar molecules form the strong sides of the ladder. The rungs of the ladder are created by weak chemical bonds between the bases. Chemical rules govern how the bases bond. For example, A always bonds with T, and G always bonds with C.

DISCOVERING THE GENETIC CODE

By 1953, scientists had identified that genes are bits of DNA that carry a code instructing the cell how to create proteins. However, they couldn't read the code. By 1961, scientists had determined that the nucleotides in DNA were arranged in groups of three, which they called codons. A codon instructs the cell to insert an amino acid, one of the building blocks of proteins. Scientists then set out to determine which codon corresponds to which amino acid.

Biochemist Marshall W. Nirenberg identified the codon for one amino acid in 1962. Soon after, scientists identified the codons for all 20 amino acids in the proteins of living organisms. Now they could begin to understand each gene's function and eventually recognize a mutation by its nucleotide sequence.

Mutations often make it less likely an organism will survive or reproduce. On rare occasions, however, mutations improve an organism's chance of survival and reproduction. In a complex species such as humans, most mutations affect only the individual in which they occur. Mutations are passed on to offspring only if they occur in the gametes, or the cells that produce eggs in biological females and sperm in biological males.

However, because of the way microbes—archaea, bacteria, and viruses—reproduce, any mutation can be passed on. So, how do microbes reproduce, anyway?

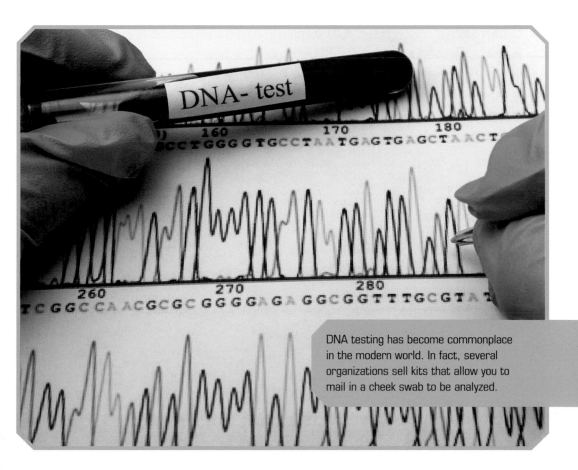

DNA testing has become commonplace in the modern world. In fact, several organizations sell kits that allow you to mail in a cheek swab to be analyzed.

MICROSCOPIC REPRODUCTION

There are two basic types of reproduction—sexual and asexual. Many microbes, including archaea and bacteria, generally reproduce asexually. Others reproduce sexually, and some can even reproduce both ways. Viruses are a special case, since they reproduce only inside living cells.

Asexual reproduction only requires a single parent. Microbes mostly reproduce through a form of asexual reproduction called binary fission, during which the microbe copies its genome and splits into two identical cells. Yeasts and some other microbes reproduce through budding. A cell produces a bud, or a small, attached growth. The "daughter" cell is a genetic duplicate of the "mother" cell and eventually breaks off. Some microbes can also reproduce through fragmentation, during which the parent cell breaks into pieces, or fragments. Each fragment grows into a complete new microbe.

This diagram shows a bacterium undergoing the process of binary fission, which results in two identical bacteria cells.

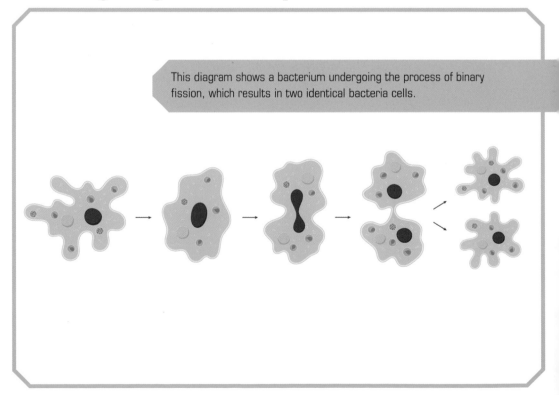

GENETIC TRAILBLAZERS

Francis Crick was born in Northampton, England, in 1916. He studied at University College, London, and Cambridge University. In 1949, he began working at Cambridge University's Cavendish Laboratory in England. James Watson was born in Chicago, Illinois, in 1928. He studied at the University of Chicago and Indiana University. In 1951, he began working at the Cavendish Laboratory , where he met Francis Crick.

After Watson's arrival, the two began working together to determine DNA's structure. Their double-helix model earned them (and biophysicist Maurice Wilkins of King's College, London) the 1962 Nobel Prize in Physiology or Medicine. Crick was later the driving force in the development of the field of molecular biology. He died in 2004. Watson was a leader in the Human Genome Project (the international effort to sequence the human genome), which he headed at the National Institutes of Health until 1992.

WHY IT MATTERS

Since the 1970s, the study of genetics has advanced by leaps and bounds. Scientists developed recombinant DNA technology. Using this process, genes from one organism are inserted into another, creating unique and often helpful traits in offspring. Experiments using the technology have enabled scientists to learn more about genes' structure and function. It has also allowed people to create superior crops and even medications.

The next big development was genome sequencing. This is the process of determining the sequence, or order, of the nucleotides in an organism's DNA and identifying the genes. In 1977, scientists sequenced the genomes of two viruses. In 1984, scientists sequenced the first virus that causes illness in humans, the Epstein-Barr virus. *Haemophilus influenzae* became the first bacterium sequenced in 1995. The following year, the first archaean (*Methano-coccus jannaschii*) was sequenced. The first protist—*Cyanidioschyzon merolae*, a unicellular red alga— was sequenced in 2004.

You might wonder why genome sequencing matters. It helps scientists understand individual species and clarifies relationships between species. Genomes also provide insight into the evolutionary history of organisms and improves our understanding of how organisms work. It can help scientists and doctors better understand the genetic causes of diseases, resulting in better diagnosis and treatment methods.

Understanding the genomes of disease-causing microbes may lead to new treatments for the illnesses they cause. Knowing the genomes of beneficial microbes may lead to improved ways to use them. Finally, remember the concept of conservation of genes across species discussed in the introduction? Whether people like it or not, humans and microbes share DNA. What scientists learn from microbes can increase our knowledge of human beings.

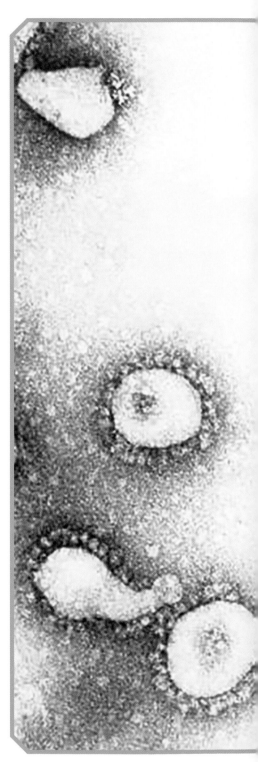

This is a transmission electron micrograph (TEM) image of coronavirus cells, taken in 1981. This coronavirus is similar to the one that caused the COVID-19 pandemic of 2020.

CHAPTER 2

THE MICROSCOPIC MENAGERIE

The traditional taxonomy system for organisms, which is no longer used by evolutionary biologists, has eight main levels, or taxa. Each level is smaller (lower) than the one before (above) it. The highest taxon, the domain, includes three categories: Bacteria, Archaea, and Eukarya (sometimes called Eukaryota). The first two are entirely microbes, and the third includes some microbes. Cell features are important factors in determining the domain in which an organism is listed. There are two basic types of cells: eukaryotic and prokaryotic. The domain Eukarya contains eukaryotic unicellular protists as well as multicellular protists, fungi, plants, and animals. Plants and animals (including humans) have eukaryotic cells. A thin membrane surrounds the cytoplasm, which contains the nucleus and small structures called organelles. The organelles perform various important functions. The nucleus is the cell's control center. It is surrounded by a membrane that protects the chromosomes.

Bacteria and archaea are prokaryotic unicellular organisms. Prokaryotic cells are much smaller than eukaryotic cells. Most have a cell wall around the cell membrane. They contain cytoplasm but have no nucleus. Instead, they have a nucleoid, which lacks a surrounding membrane. Bacteria and archaea are grouped together in the kingdom Monera.

The observant reader will have noticed that viruses haven't been mentioned. These tiny, simple organisms are major causes of disease. Where do they fit in the classification system? Keep reading to learn more.

EUKARYOTIC CELL

PROKARYOTIC CELL

These diagrams show the difference between eukaryotic cells and prokaryotic cells.

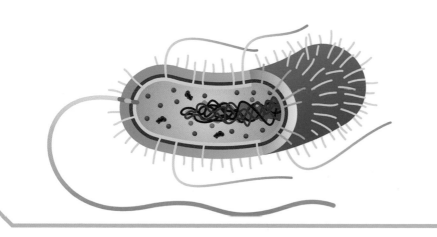

BACTERIA UP CLOSE

Bacteria are probably this first microscopic creatures you might think of. Bacteria (once called "eubacteria," meaning "true bacteria") may be spherical, rod shaped, or spiral. They may have a whipping structure used for locomotion called a flagella. Some exist as groups linked together. Bacteria live everywhere! They can be found on and in soil, in the oceans, and inside plants and animals. There are millions of them on and inside you right now, and most of them are beneficial bacteria.

Bacteria are among Earth's oldest life-forms. Billions of years ago, Earth had a very different environment. Bacteria that could thrive in extreme environments populated the planet. Extreme environments include those that are much hotter, colder, or saltier than most modern life-forms could endure. Extreme forms of bacteria still exist, which means bacteria can be found even where scientists once thought nothing could survive. Some species thrive in steaming hot springs, ice, and solid rocks. Compared to such astounding adaptability, humans are frail creatures.

People usually consider bacteria as enemies that need to be destroyed to keep us safe and well. It's true that some cause terrible, even fatal, diseases, but most are either harmless or beneficial. Bacteria have helped create an environment on Earth that makes human life possible. Many bacteria live inside humans without causing harm. Others perform vital functions without which people wouldn't survive. In fact, without those bacteria that generated oxygen gas by photosynthesis, there would never have been people.

Streptococcus pyogenes, shown here, is a species of bacteria responsible for many kinds of illnesses in humans. It can cause rashes and strep throat. It can also cause more severe and even deadly infections.

MICROSCOPIC FUNGI

The domain Eukarya includes fungi as well as protists. When most people hear the word "fungi" they usually think of organisms such as mushrooms. However, most fungi are microscopic.

You are probably familiar with microscopic fungi even if you don't realize it. Yeasts, for example, belong to this group. Some cause illnesses in animals and plants, but others are beneficial. Many people, in fact, consume yeast daily. It's an essential ingredient in making bread and beer.

You have likely seen mold growing on fruit or bread, so it may surprise you to learn that molds can also be microscopic. What people see on fruit or bread is a colony, not an individual mold. Like yeasts, molds can be beneficial or they can cause disease. Some are used in making cheese and other foods. Others yield medicines such as penicillin.

ARCHAEA UP CLOSE

When they were first discovered, archaea were widely considered strange bacteria; they were called archaebacteria. Archaea weren't even recognized as distinct from bacteria until the late 1970s. However, genetic studies later revealed that their ancestors diverged from bacteria nearly 4 billion years ago. Since the existing classification system had no place for them, scientists created the domain Archaea.

Archaea may be spherical, rod shaped, or even square or triangular. They may have flagella. Archaea live everywhere. Some, know as extremophiles (lovers of extremes), are perhaps the most famous because they live in extreme areas where other life-forms could never survive. They inhabit solid ice and steaming, sometimes highly acidic, hot springs. They live deep inside Earth's rocky surface, beneath the hottest desert sands, and in the thin, cold atmosphere high above Earth. They even can be found in oil wells and methane pools. Some live in the digestive systems of animals, including humans.

Archaea dominated the planet for Earth's first 3 billion years. These were extremophiles that could thrive in the extreme conditions that existed back then. Archaea are still extremely common. They may, in fact, be the most common microbes in the soil today. Chapter 5 examines archaea more closely.

The brilliant colors of Morning Glory hot spring in Yellowstone National Park are caused by archaea thermophiles.

BRANCHING OUT ON EARTH

This diagram shows a very simple version of the tree of life, which shows how different groups of organisms are related and when groups separated. Many branches are not shown. A tree showing all organisms would be much, much larger. Also, new discoveries and new ways of thinking will force changes to the tree and generate disagreements among biologists. Charles Darwin produced an early tree of life diagram in the mid-1800s. Modern diagrams often don't look like trees, but they're still meant to show relationships among groups of organisms.

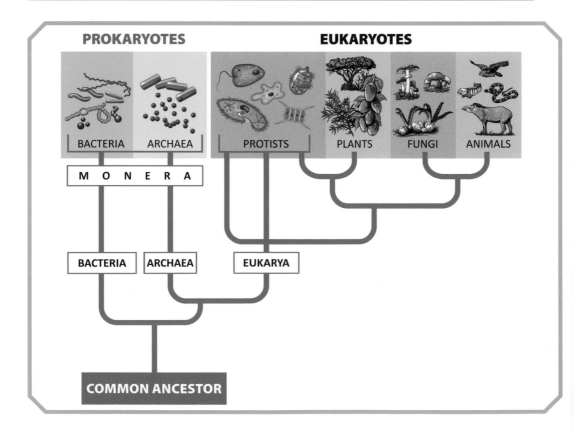

PROTISTS UP CLOSE

Protists belong to the domain Eukarya and possess typical eukaryotic cells. Familiar protists include algae and protozoans. Most protists are microscopic, unicellular organisms. Like other microbes, they live almost everywhere. Some live independently, and some have a symbiotic lifestyle, meaning they interact closely with another species and both help each other survive. Others are disease-causing parasites.

Protists are an odd group. In the late 1900s, biologists assigned numerous eukaryotes to the kingdom Protista, whose name means "the very first." They believed these organisms were primitive beings that first appeared about 2 billion years ago. Genome analysis, however, has shown that the ancestors of some protists were more complex than the modern organisms. Evidence shows that many protists aren't closely related to each other and don't really belong together in a single kingdom. But they don't belong with any other eukaryotes either. They're not animals, plants, or fungi. So, for the sake of convenience, scientists continue to use the terms "Protista" and "protist." Chapter 6 offers a closer look at protists.

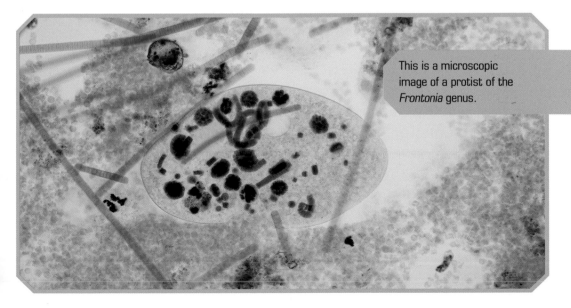

This is a microscopic image of a protist of the *Frontonia* genus.

VIRUSES UP CLOSE

Viruses are unlike other microbes. Although they're found everywhere and come in many shapes, much like bacteria and archaea, almost all viruses cause diseases in humans, other animals, plants, and even bacteria. Their definition also distinguishes them from other microbes. A virus is defined as a microscopic organism that lives inside a cell of another organism, called the host. The key words here are "lives inside." That's because a virus can only reproduce—an essential property of living things—when it's inside another organism's cell. This is because of its structure.

A virus isn't composed of cells or even a single cell. It consists solely of a nucleic acid core and a protein sheath, or coating. Without cytoplasm and its contents, it lacks the tools to reproduce. So, in order to multiply, a virus takes over the organelles of another organism's cell to carry out this function. A few viruses seem to do this without harming their host. Usually, however, viruses make the host ill, sometimes fatally.

Because of viruses' primitive structure, scientists can't agree whether they're living or not. Many consider viruses to have *both* living and nonliving characteristics.

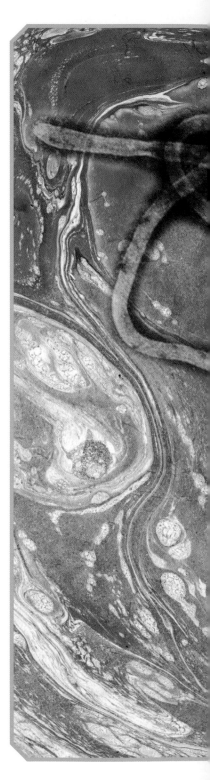

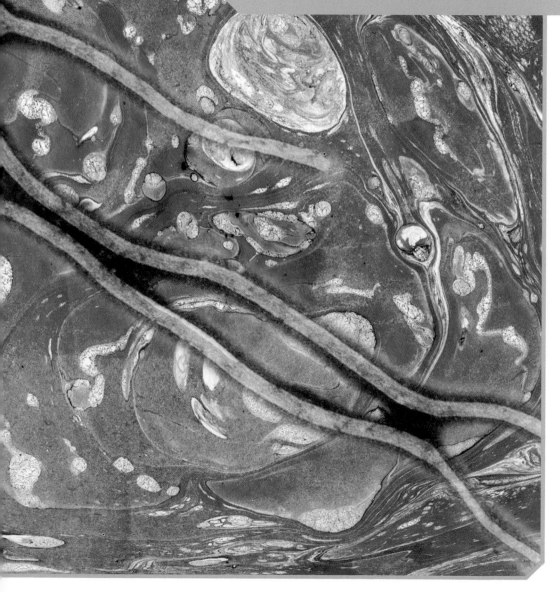

The Ebola virus, shown here, causes illness in humans and nonhuman primates. This virus is transmitted through direct contact with blood, body fluids, and animal tissues. Symptoms may include fever, headaches, body pains, weakness, abdominal pain, diarrhea, unexplained bleeding, and death.

CHAPTER 3

THE HISTORY OF MICROBIOLOGY

Microbiology is the study of microscopic organisms or micro-organisms—or microbes. Because microbiology requires microscopes, its history encompasses that of microscopes. The history of microscopes began with the earliest lenses.

Around 4,600 years age, the ancient Egyptians made lenses from rock crystal. The ancient Chinese used lenses consisting of water in a tube about 4,000 years ago. Wearable eyeglasses weren't invented until the late 1200s. Around 1590, Dutch eyeglass maker Zacharias Janssen invented the compound microscope. His invention combined the power of two or more sets of lenses. Now scientists could explore a whole new world.

PIONEERS IN MICROSCOPY

Robert Hooke and Antoni van Leeuwenhoek are two import-ant scientists in early microbiology. Both men worked in the second half of the 1600s. Hooke gave us the word "cell." Leeu-wenhoek was one of the first to see microbes. Their discoveries transformed our understanding of the world.

English experimental scientist Hooke created an illu-minated compound microscope. It was one of the most powerful microscopes of the time. Hooke often left experiments unfinished, but he contributed to numerous scientific fields. In the field of biology, Hooke's reputation is based largely on his 1665 book *Micrographia*. This guide contains written descriptions of what Hooke observed through his microscope. He coined the word "cell" to describe the tiny compartments he saw when he examined a slice of cork under his microscope. The book also contains highly detailed engravings based on Hooke's drawings of the world his microscope revealed.

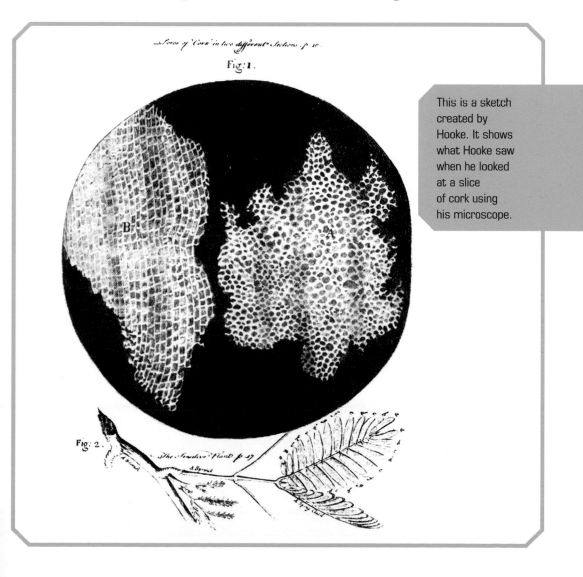

This is a sketch created by Hooke. It shows what Hooke saw when he looked at a slice of cork using his microscope.

Antoni van Leeuwenhoek wasn't a scientist. He was a Dutch cloth merchant. Oddly enough, his extraordinary scientific discoveries resulted from his humble profession. Leeuwenhoek used lenses to inspect cloth. He became a highly skilled lens maker and created simple microscopes with his lenses. Although difficult to use, their magnification was about 10 times greater than similar compound microscopes of the time. Leeuwenhoek used his microscope to discover tiny organisms he called "animalcules" ("tiny animals"). He was the first to see protozoans and to clearly describe bacteria and red blood cells. Leeuwenhoek's descriptions are so accurate that most are instantly recognizable to scientists today.

This is a replica of one of Leeuwenhoek's microscopes.

SPONTANEOUS GENERATION

Since ancient times, people once believed the idea that some life-forms sprang from nonliving matter. For example, people once thought maggots generated spontaneously in raw meat, even though they clearly saw flies buzzing around the meat. The same beliefs were held about the mold that grew on food.

Leeuwenhoek hoped his discovery of animalcules would disprove the theory of spontaneous generation. Yet people couldn't let go of the long-held theory, and belief in spontaneous generation lasted until the mid-1800s, when the work of several notable scientists disproved the outdated theory.

SUPER SCIENTISTS AND THE BATTLE AGAINST DISEASE

Prior to introduction of the first microscopes, people believed illnesses resulted from miasmas—bad air from swamps, dead bodies, and such. Leeuwenhoek suggested the animalcules he discovered were the cause. Known as the germ theory, this idea had been formulated more than a century earlier, before microbes were discovered. Italian doctor Girolamo Fracastoro had suggested that tiny "seeds" spread infectious diseases, but he lacked proof. In fact, even Leeuwenhoek's discovery wasn't enough. Belief in miasmas lasted until the mid-1800s.

English doctor Edward Jenner (1749–1823) regularly confronted smallpox, which is a viral disease that covers the body with painful, pus-filled bumps called pustules, or pox. Over the centuries, smallpox killed hundreds of millions of people and permanently harmed millions more. Although viruses were still unknown, Jenner found a safe, effective way to prevent smallpox. Today, the virus exists only in research laboratories.

Farm workers who caught a minor disease called cowpox seemed immune to smallpox. In 1796, Jenner took the pus from a worker's cowpox pustule and inserted it into cuts on a healthy boy's arm. The boy caught cowpox but recovered. Then, Jenner inserted smallpox matter into the boy's arm. The boy remained healthy because the cowpox made him immune to smallpox. Jenner called the treatment "vaccination," from the Latin word for cow, vacca.

French chemist Louis Pasteur (1822–1895) earned his fame from his work with microbes. In 1857, Pasteur proved microbes cause fermentation. This is an essential process in producing foods such as wine, beer, yogurt, and cheese. Pasteur found that some microbes function only when oxygen is absent from the environment around them. He called organisms that require oxygen "aerobic," and organisms that don't need oxygen to function, "anaerobic."

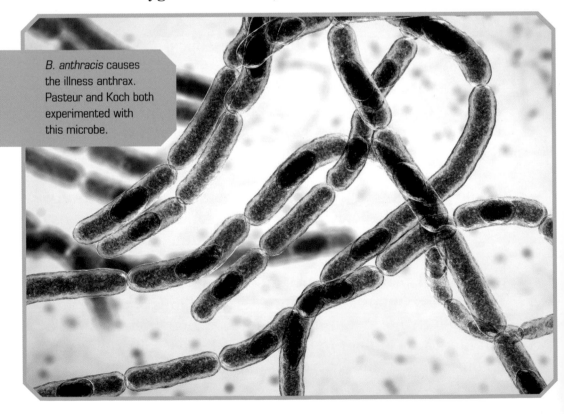

B. anthracis causes the illness anthrax. Pasteur and Koch both experimented with this microbe.

In 1859, Pasteur disproved spontaneous generation. In 1863, he developed the use of heat to kill food-spoiling microbes. Today this process is named after him—pasteurization. In 1879, Pasteur proved germ theory by demonstrating that the bacterium *Bacillus anthracis* causes the illness anthrax. Two years later, he had produced an effective anthrax vaccine. He began studying rabies in 1882. Pasteur couldn't see the virus that causes rabies, but this didn't stop him from developing an experimental vaccine in 1885 when desperate parents begged him to try it on their young son. A rabid dog had bitten the boy. Pasteur agreed to vaccinate the boy, and he saved the child's life.

Although less famous than Pasteur, German physician Robert Koch (1843–1910) was equally important in making progress in the field of microbiology. Although neither man knew it, Koch was studying anthrax at the same time Pasteur was. Both men demonstrated that *Bacillus anthracis* causes anthrax.

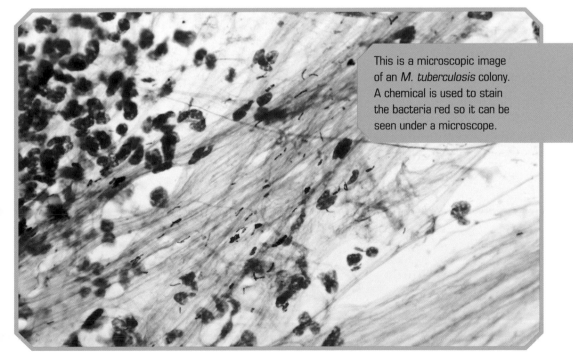

This is a microscopic image of an *M. tuberculosis* colony. A chemical is used to stain the bacteria red so it can be seen under a microscope.

In 1877, Koch published his method for preparing bacteria for study under a microscope. He also outlined a series of steps for determining if a particular microbe causes a particular disease. These steps, known as Koch's postulates, are still used by scientists today.

In 1882, Koch discovered that the bacterium *Mycobacterium tuberculosis* causes the often-fatal disease tuberculosis. In 1883, he identified the bacterium *Vibrio cholerae* as the cause of cholera. Koch received the 1905 Nobel Prize in Physiology or Medicine for his work with tuberculosis.

Surgery was very risky before the 1860s. Infections often followed even minor operations, and nearly half of all surgery patients died. English doctor Joseph Lister (1827–1912) changed that. After Pasteur's discoveries, Lister realized microbes caused infections following surgery. He insisted that antiseptics be used on hands, instruments, and bandages to kill the germs that cause infections. These practices immediately reduced the number of deaths that resulted from surgical procedures.

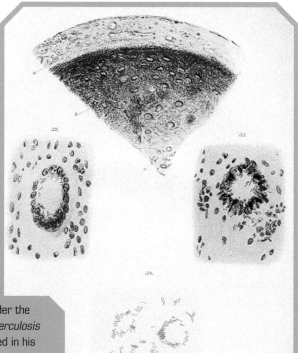

Koch often drew what he saw under the microscope, including the *M. tuberculosis* bacteria. This illustration appeared in his 1882 book *Die Ätiologie der Tuberkulose* (*The Etiology of Tuberculosis*).

KOCH'S POSTULATES

Koch developed his postulates while studying the effects of anthrax bacteria on mice.

1. The microbes must appear in a large amount in each organism infected by the disease.
2. The microbe must be able to be removed from the diseased organism and grown in a petri dish.
3. The cultured microbe should cause disease when introduced to a healthy organism.
4. The microbes in the newly infected animal must be isolated and compared to the microbes from the petri dish to prove they are the same.

THE SEARCH GOES ON

Despite the progress, scientists couldn't find causes for illnesses such as measles, yellow fever, smallpox, and rabies. Remember that Jenner and Pasteur didn't know what caused smallpox and rabies, even though they were successful in developing vaccines. Other diseases with unknown causes destroyed livestock and crops.

In 1898, Dutch microbiologist Martinus Beijerinck was researching a disease that affected tobacco crops. He strained the liquid from diseased leaves through a filter whose tiny pores prevented the passage of all known bacteria. However, the filtered liquid still spread the disease. Beijerinck called the disease-causing agent a living, liquid "virus," from a Latin word for poison. Dmitri Ivanovski, a Russian biologist, was also studying the disease. He concluded the agent was not a liquid but an extremely tiny particle. Whatever it was, no microscope of the time was powerful enough to reveal it. That would eventually change.

MODERN MICROBIOLOGY

Advances in microbiology in the early 1900s transformed the way scientists think about the origin and development of life. Progress in the study of genetics, discussed in chapter 1, played an important role, as did the developments in microscopes. In 1931, the electron microscope was introduced to the world. By bombarding an object being studied with electrons, an electron microscope can magnify objects up to 1 million times! However, because objects must be put into a vacuum, living cells can't be examined.

Shown here is an early transmission electron microscope (TEM). It's now on display at a museum in Munich, Germany.

The ion microscope was invented in 1951. It allowed scientists to look at individual atoms. In the early 1980s, people created two new microscopes. The environmental scanning electron microscope may someday allow scientists to study living cells. The scanning tunneling microscope allowed researchers to take three-dimensional images of metal surfaces at an atomic level. More recently, digital microscopes have been used to send images directly to computer screens.

During this new era of microscopic technology, other scientists developed new ideas and discovered new categories of microbes. In 1957, when Russia launched Sputnik I, the first satellite, most scientists thought life in the extreme environment of space was impossible. Microbiologist Joshua Lederberg disagreed. He speculated about what would happen if astronauts brought alien microbes back to Earth. Then, in 1992, physicist Thomas Gold argued that billions of microbes could be found in Earth's interior. Most scientists at the time considered this idea absurd, but it's now considered fact. What changed? Extremophiles were discovered.

Starting in the 1960s, scientists discovered many microbes in extreme environments. This include hot springs, deep-ocean vents where water temperature and pressure are extremely high, and extremely cold places. Then, in the 1970s, something else astounding happened. Microbiologist Carl Woese determined that many of these extremophiles belonged to an entirely new domain—Archaea. Once again, our knowledge of microbes was turned upside down, and scientists continue to make discoveries about the microscopic world all around us.

CHAPTER 4

BACTERIA

Bacteria are one of Earth's oldest life-forms. Scientists know this because of the fossils they've left behind. Yes, even microbes can leave fossils. Earth's oldest known fossils are 3.5-billion-year-old prokaryotes.

According to physician and researcher Frank Lowy, bacteria range in size from about 0.2 to 10 micrometers.. How small is that? One inch equals more than 25,000 micrometers! Bacteria may be shaped like spheres (cocci), rods (bacilli), or spirals (spirillum). Thousands of bacteria species are known, and millions may exist.

While these are the three main bacteria forms, other shapes are possible. Some are shaped like a corkscrew, and some form long filaments.

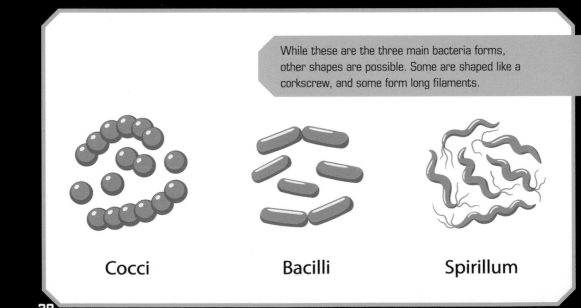

Cocci   Bacilli   Spirillum

Most species of bacteria are very versatile. Some, known as extremophiles, can even be found in places where life seems impossible. Extremophiles live in ice and around deep-sea vents, where temperatures exceed the boiling point of water and the water pressure is crushing. Billions of bacteria dwell deep inside Earth, without air and sunlight. These are known as "SLIMEs," which stands for subterranean lithoautotrophic microbial ecosystems. "Subterranean" means below Earth's surface. "Lithoautotrophic" means getting its energy from minerals rather than organic material.

It's hard to say how many bacteria exist at one time on Earth. They live in colonies in the millions and can reproduce quickly. In *Deadly Companions*, Crawford writes that a single ounce (30 ml) of seawater contains at least 30 million bacteria!

This is a close-up image of bacteria that live near a hot spring.

BENEFICIAL BACTERIA

You've most likely seen advertisements on television or in stores for antibacterial products. The message is clear: Bacteria are bad. However, the fact is that most bacteria are harmless or even helpful to humans.

In fact, ancient bacteria helped make all eukaryotic life on Earth possible. Billions of years ago, when the first bacteria appeared, Earth was much hotter and its atmosphere lacked oxygen. Early bacteria called cyanobacteria changed conditions by performing photosynthesis and releasing oxygen as a waste product. Modern bacteria still do many useful things.

Eventually, all organisms die. If the life cycle stopped there, however, dead organisms would cover the planet. The essential nutrients living organisms need to stay alive would be trapped in the dead organisms. New life couldn't begin. Luckily for us and other organisms, decomposers—notably bacteria and fungi—break down dead organisms and release the nutrients to be reused. One of these critical nutrients is nitrogen.

All organisms need nitrogen in order to build amino acids and DNA. Earth's atmosphere has plenty of nitrogen; in fact it's the most common gas in the atmosphere. However, plants and animals can't use gaseous nitrogen. Bacteria help by performing a process called nitrogen fixation. Decomposers release ammonia, and other bacteria change ammonia into nitrogen compounds called nitrites. Plants get nitrogen from nitrates, and animals get it from plants.

People may be unaware that they eat good bacteria daily. Bacteria are used to make some of our most basic foods. For example, bread requires bacteria as well as yeast. Dairy foods such as cheese, butter, and yogurt need bacteria too. Bacteria are used to make kefir, a fermented milk product popular in many areas of the world. Bacteria are also used to make sausage, sauerkraut, miso, and soy sauce. Perhaps most surprising is that bacteria help create many people's favorite sweet—chocolate!

Bacteria provide numerous other benefits. The ones that feast on human and animal waste are used to clean wastewater. Others eat oil and are used to clean up oil spills. Bacteria help control insect pests too. Drug companies use bacteria to make medicines and vitamins. They even make antibiotics from bacteria! Many researchers are investigating other beneficial uses for bacteria. These include fighting health problems such as intestinal disorders and cancer and producing fuel. Perhaps someday bacteria will power cars!

Gardeners who make compost for their gardens rely on bacteria to help break down organic material to create a healthy planting medium.

DETRIMENTAL BACTERIA

Many of the species of bacteria that aren't beneficial to humans are bad for us. "Bad" bacteria cause infections and diseases that range from mild to fatal. They cause infection in cuts, sore throats, and ear infections. Some can cause a bad case of food poisoning, while other cause cholera, pneumonia, tuberculosis, and even stomach ulcers.

Heat can be used to kill many bacteria. We use disinfectants to destroy bacteria in water and on surfaces. We use antiseptics to prevent infection in cuts and wounds. Doctors may give vaccines to prevent bacterial diseases or prescribe antibiotics to treat them. The overuse of antibiotics, however, has created drug-resistant bacteria. This means infections and diseases that were once easy to treat can now become quite serious. The disease MRSA (Methicillin-resistant *Staphylococcus aureus*) can cause a range of symptoms, from a rash and blisters to pneumonia. Left untreated, MRSA can lead to sepsis. Some forms of MRSA are highly resistant to antibiotics, and cleanliness is the best way to avoid this illness. Scientists are seeking new ways to fight these bacteria.

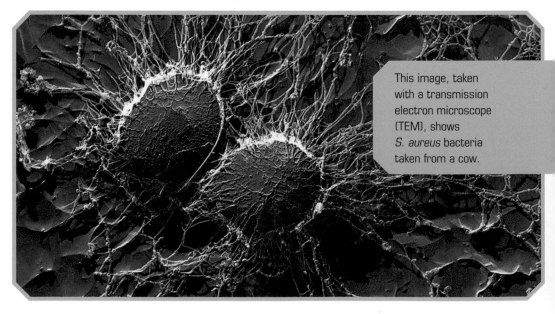

This image, taken with a transmission electron microscope (TEM), shows *S. aureus* bacteria taken from a cow.

LIVING WITH BACTERIA

In symbiosis, two organisms live in a close, mutually beneficial union. Some bacteria have symbiotic relationships with plants or animals. Remember bacteria's role in nitrogen recycling? This process produced a symbiotic relationship between bacteria and plants. Bacteria called rhizobia infect the roots of certain legumes. They give the plants nitrogen, and in return they receive nutrients for growth and a safe place to live. This form of symbiosis is called mutualism, because both species receive a benefit.

Many animals have mutualistic relationships with bacteria. For example, tiny insects called aphids eat tree sap that lacks amino acids. Bacteria inside their cells produce amino acids for the aphids; in return, the bacteria get energy and nutrients. The Hawaiian squid provides a safe home for special light-producing bacteria. The squid uses the light to camouflage itself.

People have symbiotic relationships with bacteria too. For example, bacteria inside the human mouth get nutrients from our food while protecting people from disease-causing microbes. Bacteria in human intestines receive essential nutrients while helping with digestion.

Symbiosis contributed to the development of plants and animals. Chloroplasts in plant and some protist cells and mitochondria in all eukaryotic cells produce energy. Chloroplasts are the descendants of an ancient cyanobacterium. Mitochondria are what's left of an ancient proteobacterium.

SORTING BACTERIA

Bacteria are classified in several ways. One method uses shape—cocci (spherical), bacilli (rod shaped), and spirillum (spiral). Sometimes they are sorted based on whether they're aerobic or anaerobic. Another method depends on their reaction to the Gram's stain (a purple dye). The bacteria are stained with the dye, then washed with chemicals. "Gram-positive" bacteria are thin-walled cells that remain purple. Thick-walled bacteria lose the dye and are called "gram negative." However, shape, metabolism, and Gram's staining tell us nothing about relationships among different bacteria. Therefore, the best way to properly classify bacteria is by sequencing RNA or DNA.

Animal cells contain structures called ribosomes. These are the organelles that manufacture proteins. Carl Woese used the 16s ribosomal RNA (16s rRNA) gene to classify bacteria. He chose this gene because every prokaryote has it, and it doesn't vary much among species.

The largest group of bacteria, known as Firmicutes, has nearly 2,500 species. Most are gram positive. Parasitic mycoplasma are the tiniest bacteria. Actinobacteria are decomposers. Many yield valuable antibiotics. Proteobacteria are gram negative. This large group includes *E. coli*, many disease-causing bacteria, rhizobia, and bacteria that might be closely related to mitochondria's ancestors. Bacteroidetes include the gram-negative anaerobic bacteria that inhabit the human intestine. Cyanobacteria carry out photosynthesis. One ancient cyanobacterium was the ancestor of all chloroplasts.

BACTERIAL STRUCTURE

Cell walls enclose most bacteria, just as our skin covers our bodies. The rigid walls contain a material called peptidoglycan, which is stained by the Gram's stain. Just inside the cell wall is a membrane. Gram-negative bacteria have a membrane outside the wall as well. They usually have less peptidoglycan in the wall. A slimy capsule surrounds everything.

Many bacteria have one or more flagella attached to the outside to help them move. Some bacteria also have hairlike structures called pili that help them attach to each other and to the host.

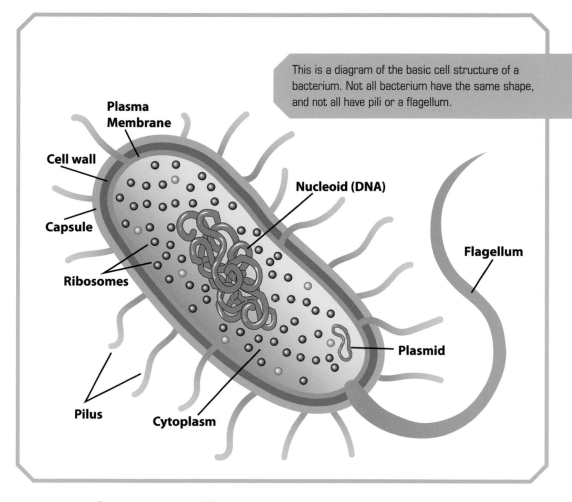

Plasma Membrane

Cell wall

Capsule

Ribosomes

Pilus

Cytoplasm

Nucleoid (DNA)

Flagellum

Plasmid

This is a diagram of the basic cell structure of a bacterium. Not all bacterium have the same shape, and not all have pili or a flagellum.

The interior is filled with a liquid called cytoplasm. It contains enzymes that help in digestion and building parts, storage bodies called inclusions, nutrients, RNA, and DNA. Within a bacterium's nucleoid is a single circular chromosome. The cytoplasm may also contain smaller DNA bits called plasmids, which often carry genes that fight antibiotics.

Most bacteria reproduce through binary fission, although cyanobacteria can use budding and fragmentation. Because bacteria reproduce asexually, they don't have special reproductive structures. However, some bacteria use pili to connect and exchange bits of DNA in a process called conjugation.

SUPER BACTERIA SKILLS

Scientific research has shown some amazing bacterial abilities. Although bacteria have rigid outer walls, they are quite elastic. They can flatten themselves to pass through extremely tiny openings, then return to their normal shape. Bacteria can also communicate by releasing chemicals into their surroundings to learn about their environment and communicate the information to other bacteria in the colony. This skill helps the colony adapt and survive.

BACTERIAL GENOMES

Scientists first sequenced a bacterial genome in 1995. Some might wonder, "So what? What difference does it make if scientists sequence bacterial genomes?" It can make a big difference.

Knowing a bacterium's genome helps scientists understand the organism. That may allow scientists discover more effective ways to fight bad bacteria and use good bacteria. Knowing bacterial genomes helps scientists understand the plants and animals that share a symbiotic relationship with bacteria. Remember, too, that cellular organelles such as mitochondria and chloroplasts began as symbiotic bacteria. Therefore, everything scientists learn about bacteria helps them understand more about all life on Earth. Finally, it was sequencing ribosomes that led Carl Woese to the discovery of archaea, changed scientists' understanding of life, and opened a new world of possibilities.

Bacterial research is an ongoing process. Scientists continue to study bacteria in the hope of discovering new uses for the microscopic creatures.

CHAPTER 5

ARCHAEA

Just like bacteria, archaea are ancient organisms. They have left behind a significant amount of fossil evidence. Huge microbial mats of archaea and bacteria covered large sections of ocean floor with odd structures. A microbial mat is an immense collection of different microbe species. Microbes form mats because microbes are much stronger and more efficient working together than as separate species.

Archaea are prokaryotes. Although originally considered weird bacteria, genetic studies have demonstrated that they're very different from bacteria; in fact, we now treat them as a separate domain. They were defined as a group in 1977, about three centuries after Leeuwenhoek observed bacteria.

It's impossible to tell how many species of archaea (or, in fact, of bacteria) there are in the world. They may exist in the millions. "Species" isn't easy to define for prokaryotes, which don't "breed" as eukaryotes do. Bulk samples of seawater and soils contain DNA fragments that most likely come from a staggering number of species. Scientists do believe that individual archaea are at least as numerous as bacteria. Tim Friend writes that a single drop of seawater holds a million or more!

Stromatolites, like those shown here, form in microbial mats. They form when certain microbes secrete a glue-like substance that creates layer upon layer of hardened material. Some scientists consider these geological structures the oldest living things on Earth.

EXTREME ARCHAEA

Archaea can be found everywhere you find bacteria. They live on Earth's surface, in the soil and oceans, and deep underground in rock. Some archaea are SLIMES (mentioned in chapter 4), just like some bacteria. Archaea also live inside people. They can be aerobic or anaerobic. Many are extremophiles, which includes thermophiles, or "lovers of heat." Some like such extremely high temperatures they're called hyperthermophiles ("hyper" means "excessively"). Archaea called psychrophiles prefer intensely cold places, such as Antarctica. Halophiles inhabit extremely salty places, such as the Dead Sea. Acidophiles like places with a low pH, which means the environment is acidic. Alkaliphiles prefer the opposite. They live where the pH is high.

You might wonder why archaea can live in so many extreme environments. For one thing, some species can "eat," or breakdown, inorganic materials such as iron, sulfur, carbon dioxide, hydrogen, ammonia, uranium, and other substances that are toxic to humans. Think about that for a minute. Archaea can use iron to make nutrients. No person could manage that feat!

The Dead Sea is about 34 percent salt. What could live in such a harsh environment? Archaea!

A NEW DOMAIN

Carl Woese published an article about archaea in 1977. After almost 10 years of research, Woese had demonstrated they were so different from bacteria and eukaryotes that they constituted a new domain. Many scientists thought Woese had to be wrong. Many felt that the idea that the tree of life had two domains—Bacteria and Eukarya—was well established and had to be correct. However, Woese's discovery forced scientists to create a new tree of life and rethink how life developed on Earth and how organisms are related to each other. It started a revolution that has not yet ended.

HOW MANY KINDS ARE THERE?

Biologists are still debating the number of major Archaea groups. At least two exist. Crenarchaeota may be the most common. This group includes the archaea living in the hottest places. One species lives in temperatures high enough to sterilize surgical instruments! Other Crenarchaeotes, called thermoacidophiles, like hot, acidic environments. Still others live in cool ocean waters. Many soil microbes that convert ammonia into nitrites also belong to Crenarchaeota.

The second major group, Euryarchaeota, has three main subgroups. The methanogens, so named because they produce methane gas, are found in anaerobic environments such as swamps, animal digestive systems, and sewage systems. Halophiles love salty habitats like the Dead Sea and salt ponds at the south end of San Francisco Bay. Euryarchaeota's thermoacidophiles don't like as much heat as Crenarchaeota's. They can be found in places like Yellowstone National Park's sulfur springs.

Biologists debate how to classify archaea in the groups Korarchaeota and Nanoarchaeota. Some believe Korarchaeota is a subbranch of Crenarchaeota. Others, however, think its members are very ancient ancestors of Crenarchaeota, Euryarchaeota, and Eukarya. Genome sequencing of Korarchaeotes revealed that one type possesses genes long believed distinctive to these other groups.

The Nanoarchaeota are very small; in fact, they're the smallest microbes yet discovered. This is why they're called "nano" (which means one-billionth of something). Most are about 400 nanometers in diameter. How small is that? The head of a pin has a diameter of about 1 million nanometers! Nanoarchaeota seem to be parasites, but they lack genes for digestion.

ARCHAEAN STRUCTURE

Archaea resemble bacteria in many ways. That's why they were first considered weird bacteria. A membrane and cell wall surround most archaea, and a capsule encloses everything. A flagellum and pili may be attached to the outside. The interior holds cytoplasm with ribosomes, a nucleoid, plasmids, and storage bodies. Storage bodies in archaea are called granules rather than inclusions, as the storage bodies in bacteria are called.

If they're so similar, how do we know that archaea are different from bacteria? Archaea have some distinctive shapes. Some are spheres, rods, or spirals, like bacteria, but others form extremely thin filaments. Some rod-shaped archaea are almost perfect rectangles. One species is flat and square. Others are triangular. Some have no cell wall to hold a shape, so they have an irregular shape similar to an amoeba.

Archaea are different from bacteria in important chemical ways. For example, their cell walls lack the peptidoglycan in bacteria cell walls. Archaean membranes and flagella contain different chemicals, and their storage bodies hold different material. Archaean ribosomes act more like those of humans than those of bacteria

THE GENETICS OF ARCHAEA

In addition to the differences mentioned above, archaea also differ from bacteria genetically. In 1996, scientists finished sequencing the first archaean genome for *Methanococcus jannaschii*. As more archaea were sequenced, scientists learned that microbes contain many genes not found in bacteria or eukaryotes. They also discovered that archaean genomes contain inactive DNA segments called introns. These segments exist in eukaryotes but not in bacteria. In addition, scientists found that the process by which archaea utilize DNA and RNA

This is an artist's depiction of *Pyrococcus furiosus*, a species of archaea that lives in very hot environments.

to produce proteins resembles that in eukaryotes more than that in bacteria.

As in bacteria, archaean reproduction occurs through binary fission, budding, or fragmentation. These forms of asexual reproduction limit genetic variation in a species. However, archaea also exchange plasmids using a process similar to conjugation in bacteria. As scientists learned more about microbial genetics, they discovered that archaea can actually transfer genes from one organism to another! This occurs between organisms within one domain but also, remarkably, between organisms in different domains as well. Archaea genes can transfer not just from one organism to a similar one but from one organism to a very different one. This phenomenon is called horizontal, or lateral, gene transfer. It still occurs and has huge implications for understanding the beginning and development of life on Earth.

CHAPTER 6

PROTISTA — PROTOZOANS, ALGAE, AND MORE

Protists are eukaryotes. They make up almost all unicellular organisms that aren't prokaryotes (such as yeasts). As Chapter 2 noted, modern science has shown they're not closely related. Protists include a remarkable variety of organisms. Some protists were formerly considered plants, animals, or fungi, while others hadn't even been discovered before the term "protist" was invented. Most protists are unicellular. Unlike other eukaryotes, multicellular protists have only one kind of tissue. Still, the organisms aren't closely related. Scientists continue to use the terms "protist" and "Protista" simply because it's easier than saying "eukaryotes that aren't animals, plants, or fungi."

THE LIFE OF A PROTIST

Similar to other microbes, protists are among Earth's oldest life-forms. Early forms of algae helped increase the amount of oxygen in Earth's atmosphere. This made the development of modern life-forms possible.

Scientists have discovered about 200,000 protist species, and millions more may exist. Protists may be free living, symbiotic, or parasitic. Free-living forms fill oceans, freshwater bodies, swimming pools, and sewage treatment plants. They can also be found in soil, forest floors, deserts, and trees. Symbiotic protists live in close contact with animals, plants, fungi, and even other protists. Hundreds of thousands of protists may live in the gut of a single termite. Parasitic protists harm animals and plants.

Many protists are able to create energy through the process of photosynthesis, but others get their energy from food. Most protists are aerobic. However, parasites as well as some other species live where they must be able to function anaerobically.

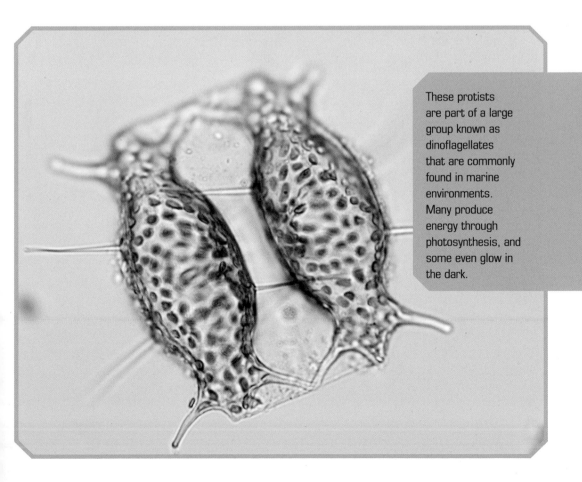

These protists are part of a large group known as dinoflagellates that are commonly found in marine environments. Many produce energy through photosynthesis, and some even glow in the dark.

BAD PROTISTS AND GOOD PROTISTS

A parasitic protist causes the disease malaria. Malaria is treatable today, but it is otherwise a deadly disease. Biologist John Kimball estimates it has killed more people than any other infectious disease. Although the treatment for malaria is effective, it's not always readily available to people everywhere. The CDC has reported that, in 2019, there were an estimated 229 million cases of malaria worldwide, and 409,000 people died from it. Most deaths occurred to children in African countries.

Protists in the genus *Plasmodium* infect people with malaria. This 3D rendering shows *Plasmodium* cells (green) attacking red blood cells.

Other parasitic protists cause sickness in humans and various animal diseases. African Trypanosomiasis—also called "sleeping sickness"—is caused by a protist transmitted by the tsetse fly. Some fungus-like protists attack plants. In Ireland during the 1840s, a protist destroyed potato crops and caused a famine. Another protist killed so many grapes in France that it nearly ruined the French wine industry.

However, many protists are beneficial. They help maintain the atmospheric balance of oxygen and carbon dioxide. They're important marine decomposers and nutrient recyclers. Symbiotic protists inside coral animals make spectacular coral reefs possible. Coral reefs are home to a rich variety of life-forms. Some marine protists leave behind shells that help create limestone, which people use in construction.

There are a number of distinct protist groups, which are only distantly related to each other. Let's look at several to get some sense of their variety and complexity.

FIRST ANIMALS

Scientists first thought of protists as simple animals from which later animals evolved. In fact, "protozoa" means "first animals." Some protists have animal-like features such as a mouth or an eyespot that senses light and dark. Some contain the pigment chlorophyll and are able to carry out photosynthesis just like plants. Today, scientists no longer consider protozoans to belong to a single group and don't use the term in the scientific classification system. However, the term is still widely used for general audiences.

There are tens of thousands of protist species. They live in moist places. Millions live in bodies of water where they recycle nutrients and clean the water by eating bacteria. In turn, they serve as food for other small organisms.

There are numerous ways of categorizing protozoans, because they come in so many shapes and structures. They may be grouped based on how they move. For example, flagellates use flagella to move. Sarcodines move by means of pseudopods, or false feet, which they form by creating fingerlike projections. Apicomplexans move by gliding. The most complex protozoans are the ciliates. Fine hairlike cilia cover them, helping them move and capture food. Paramecia, science-class favorites, are ciliates.

Some protozoans have chloroplasts and conduct photosynthesis. Others feed on other organisms. Some are parasites, such as the flagellate that causes African Trypanosomiasis. Amoebas and foraminifera (the protists whose shells help form limestone) belong to this group. Parasites, including the malaria parasite, also belong to this group.

WHAT ARE ALGAE?

Algae are simple organisms inhabiting saltwater, freshwater, and moist soil. Some species are very large. For example, kelp can grow to about 200 feet (60 m) long. However, the focus here is on microscopic algae. Unlike "protozoa," "algae" is a useful descriptive term, but it's important to understand that the organisms called "algae" aren't closely related.

Algae have chloroplasts and carry out photosynthesis. They provide much of the world's oxygen and form the bottom of the food chain for nearly all marine and freshwater life. Depending on the pigment in their chloroplasts, algae may be red, green, or brown. Microscopic algae are usually green. Most live in freshwater. Algae come in many shapes. Some have two or more flagella, while others have none. One tiny symbiotic type has become a popular health food because of its rich protein and chlorophyll content.

Other microscopic algae include freshwater golden algae. Most are photosynthetic, but they may feed on other microbes when there's insufficient light. Diatoms get a golden-brown color from their green and yellow-orange pigments. They differ

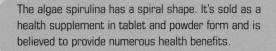

The algae spirulina has a spiral shape. It's sold as a health supplement in tablet and powder form and is believed to provide numerous health benefits.

from other algae in having a hard, glasslike skeleton made of silica. Frustules come in a variety of beautiful, intricate shapes.

FUNGUS, MOLD, AND SLIME

The fungus-like protists include water molds and slime molds. Water molds are very distant relatives of fungi. Slime molds, however, are unrelated to fungi, although they're distant relatives of water molds.

This is a pile of oak trees that have been infected with *Phytophthora ramorum*.

Water molds include the microbe that caused the Irish potato famine. Another form attacks grapes. Some species are parasites for fish and amphibians. Sudden oak death (SOD) is a condition caused by the water mold *Phytophthora ramorum,* which has caused extensive danage to oak forests in California and Oregon

Cellular slime molds spend most of their lives as unicellular organisms. At certain times, however, thousands gather together in a swarm. Plasmodial slime molds also have a life-cycle stage when thousands join together. Unlike their cellular cousins, however, the individual cells don't remain separate. Instead, they unite in a single giant cell with thousands of nuclei.

Some protists lack mitochondria—the organelle of eukaryotic cells that creates power—although they appear to be descendants of earlier protists that did possess mitochondria. Parasitic *Giardia*, for example, infect people's intestines and can cause diarrhea. Parabasalians that live inside animals may cause infection, coexist with the host symbiotically, or have no effect on the host. Pelobiontids rely on symbiotic bacteria to compensate for their missing mitochondria.

PROTOZOAN GENETICS

Scientists still have much to learn about protists. There are many disagreements that must be resolved. Genome analysis has already revealed important information. Studies of protists that lack mitochondria suggest they may form one of the eukaryotic tree's earliest branches. The gene sequences of ciliates, apicomplexans, and dinoflagellates imply they share a common ancestor.

An important difference between water molds and fungi has been revealed through genetic analysis. The gene sequences of water molds differ significantly from those of fungi. They are much more closely related to the sequences of diatoms and golden and brown algae. Furthermore, water molds, diatoms, and brown algae have genes very similar to those in both green and red algae.

Finally, there's a group of flagellates called choanoflagellates because of a collar structure ("choano") around their flagella. Although they're unicellular, they have genes for several proteins crucial to interactions between cells in complex multicellular animals. These microbes are in fact the closest protist relatives to people.

CHAPTER 7

VIRUSES

Everyone's had a viral disease like a cold or the flu. In 2020, the entire world became aware of a particularly deadly virus: COVID-19. We know the importance of protecting ourselves and others from viral infections. Yet how much do most people really know about viruses?

Viruses are the tiniest microbes. They're invisible even with the most powerful compound microscope. The largest viral microbe is about 1/10 the size of the average bacterium. The smallest is about 0.01 micrometer long. It would take about two and a half million placed end to end to equal one inch!

Viruses have existed for millions of years. They can be found almost everywhere. They're built to live as parasites in plants, animals (including people), and bacteria. They cause deadly diseases like smallpox, AIDS, and some cancers. Even "ordinary" viral diseases, such as influenza, can be fatal. However, viruses have also played a critical role in the development of life on Earth.

What makes viruses so dangerous? Their structure is part of the reason.

IS IT ALIVE?

Viruses aren't composed of cells like other organisms. A virus is just genetic material—DNA or, sometimes, RNA—enclosed in a protein coat. There's nothing else—no cytoplasm, plasmids, ribosomes, inclusions, granules, or organelles.

Proteins called capsomeres make up the coat, or capsid, which gives the virus its shape. Some viruses have multiple sides. Some are roughly oval. Others look like long, skinny sticks or bits of string. Some even resemble a lunar landing vehicle!

The capsid protects the genetic material inside. Sometimes an additional protective envelope of proteins, fats, and carbohydrates surrounds the capsid. Sometimes these envelopes have spikes that help the virus attach to host cells.

The virus's structure presents an essential question: Are viruses alive? They can't reproduce—an activity associated with

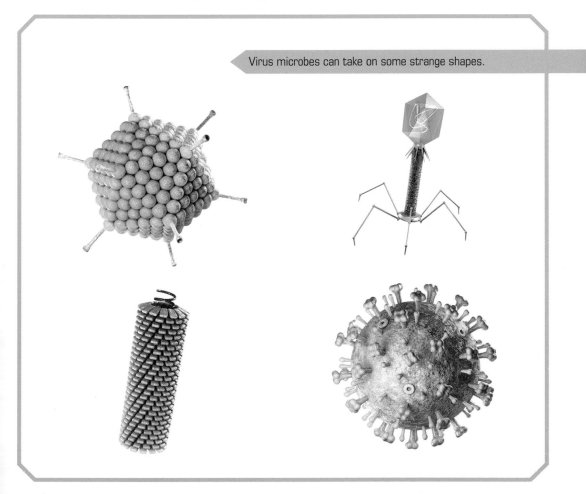

Virus microbes can take on some strange shapes.

living organisms. Once inside a host cell, however, a virus's nucleic acid takes over the cell's machinery and can reproduce rapidly. So is it alive or not? Scientists still don't agree.

HOW DO THEY WORK?

Most viruses require specific host cells. A virus recognizes its host through receptors on the host's exterior. Receptors help the virus bind to the host, and then the virus injects its nucleic acid into the host, takes command, and reproduces.

Viruses reproduce by two methods, or cycles. In the lytic cycle, the host's DNA is destroyed and the viral DNA takes over. Soon after, the cell lyses (bursts) and releases a new generation of viruses. In the lysogenic cycle, the viral DNA or RNA becomes part of the host DNA. The host cell may divide many times, carrying the viral nucleic acid, without any cell dying. While the lytic cycle causes disease in the host, the lysogenic cycle doesn't. Sometimes, however, a virus switches from the lysogenic to the lytic cycle.

Certain RNA viruses—called retroviruses—contain an enzyme called reverse transcriptase. It allows virus RNA to make a DNA copy of itself inside the host. This becomes a permanent part of the host's genome.

Because most viruses reproduce rapidly, they have a greater chance for mutations. That's a good survival mechanism for viruses because it can produce viruses resistant to traditional treatments. However, it's bad news for hosts because they're constantly attacked by new viruses.

Mutations can also enable viruses to jump from one species to another. For example, scientists examined the genes of the 2009 H1N1 (swine flu virus) after it first appeared in humans. Early tests showed it possessed genes similar to those normally seen in flu viruses of North American pigs. Further study, however, revealed two genes from flu viruses normally found

This diagram demonstrates both the lytic and lysogenic cycles. The figure-eight pattern shows that a virus can switch between the two cycles.

LYTIC CYCLE

LYSOGENIC CYCLE

in European and Asian pigs, bird genes, and human genes. This virus had jumped around a lot!

Viroids and virusoids are the smallest, simplest viruses. They're just genetic material without a capsid. Viroids cause diseases in plant cells, but their lack of a capsid makes it difficult for them to spread to another plant or even another cell. Virusoids must insert themselves into a "helper" virus to reproduce, much like viruses require host cells to reproduce.

WHAT IS A CORONAVIRUS?

The COVID-19 pandemic of 2020 made viruses a worldwide concern. However, COVID-19 is just one of many coronaviruses. All of these microbes are surrounded by spikes of proteins. This is where they get their name—"corona" is Latin for "crown."

Most coronaviruses affect the upper respiratory system in animals and humans. Some are mild. Others are deadly. They spread though droplets released into the air when someone talks, sneezes, yawns, etc. These droplets can then infect others.

Scientists have identified many coronaviruses in animals. Seven of these coronaviruses have affected humans. Four are common and cause mild colds. The other three can lead to more severe illness:

- **SEVERE ACUTE RESPIRATORY SYNDROME (SARS)** was a contagious and potentially fatal respiratory illness that affected the world from 2002 to 2003. No new cases of SARS have occurred since 2004.
- **MIDDLE EAST RESPIRATORY SYNDROME (MERS)** was first identified in Saudi Arabia in 2012. Outbreaks still occur sporadically. Scientists are still working to find a vaccination.
- **SEVERE ACUTE RESPIRATORY SYNDROME CORONAVIRUS 2 (SARS-COV-2)** causes coronavirus disease 19 (COVID-19).

BAD VIRUSES

As mentioned at the beginning of the chapter, the "common cold" is caused by a virus—or, more accurately, several. Almost 100 types of rhinovirus (from the Greek word for nose, *rhis*) exist! Researchers finally completed sequencing the DNA of those known in 2009.

Viruses also cause chicken pox, measles, and mumps. As already mentioned, they also cause influenza, or flu. Up to 60 million people in the United States get the flu annually. Most recover. However, flu can lead to more serious illnesses and even result in death. Very young children, the elderly, and people with suppressed immune systems are most at risk. That's why people are encouraged to get yearly flu shots. Thanks to the safety precautions taken by people all over the world during the COVID-19 pandemic, the number of reported cases of influenza dropped dramatically in 2020 and 2021.

Most Americans today probably aren't familiar with poliomyelitis—polio for short. This terrible viral disease once paralyzed or killed tens of thousands of people. Today, vaccines can prevent polio.

Dreadful viral diseases called hemorrhagic fevers are most common in Africa. Patients experience flulike symptoms, then develop internal and external bleeding (hemorrhaging). Up to 90 percent of patients die. Ebola is the most well known hemorrhagic fever.

Herpes viruses receive a lot of attention today. At least 25 kinds exist and at least eight infect humans. Herpes viruses cause cold sores and the disease called infectious mononucleosis. They can also cause sores on the chest, face, eyes, and sexual organs. They can even cause a serious brain infection that may be fatal.

HIV, or human immunodeficiency virus, also receives a lot of attention. It's the retrovirus that causes AIDS (acquired immunodeficiency syndrome). People with AIDS have severely weakened immune systems. They become ill easily and have difficulty fighting diseases. They are also more likely to get rare, often fatal, diseases. Scientists decoded HIV's genome in 2009.

Viruses cause hundreds of animal diseases. One example is canine distemper, which causes serious illness and sometimes death in puppies. A virus causes diseases known as foot-and-mouth (hoof-and-mouth) disease in cattle, sheep, and pigs. Infected animals develop painful blisters in and around their mouth and above their hooves. Adults rarely die, but young animals may. Viruses are also responsible for cowpox, rabies, and some animal cancers.

Viruses infect all kinds of plants too. Remember that Beijerinck and Ivanovski were studying a tobacco plant disease. Viruses also attack flowers and all sorts of fruits and vegetables. The list is almost endless.

Viruses even infect bacteria. These are called bacteriophages, or phages for short. ("Phage" comes from a Greek word meaning "one who eats.") Phages often kill their bacterial hosts, although some coexist in a lysogenic cycle. Like all microbes, phages are everywhere. According to the American Society for Microbiology, the weight of all the phages on Earth is more than 1,000 times the total weight of the world's elephant population!

CAN VIRUSES BE HELPFUL?

Believe it or not, viruses have also provided benefits. They've actually contributed to the development of life on Earth. Remember the mixture of genes in the H1N1 virus? It demonstrates how viruses redistribute genes among organisms. Because genes are the basic units of heredity, such activity shapes how organisms change and evolve.

Scientists today find viruses useful for several purposes. The scientists who study viruses are called virologists. They are working on ways to use viruses instead of insecticides to protect crops. Insecticides can harm plants and other animals. Viruses specific to particular insect pests could be used to kill them without harming other organisms. Scientists also use viruses to develop vaccines and other drugs. Viruses are also extremely useful in genetic research because of their simple structure. Biologists have used bacteriophages to study genes and DNA. Remember the discussion about conservation of genes across species at the beginning of the book? That means the research on bacteriophages gives scientists genetic knowledge that can be applied to all organisms.

Because microbes live everywhere—even in places where scientists long thought life was impossible—they help scientists develop greater understanding of life in general. Just as research on phage genetics provides insight into all organisms, so does research on the genetics of all microbes. This knowledge can help with the search for life beyond Earth. It may lead to new ideas for medical treatments, fuels, or robotics. It may lead science in directions not even imagined yet. Microbes may be tiny, but their impact on our live is huge.

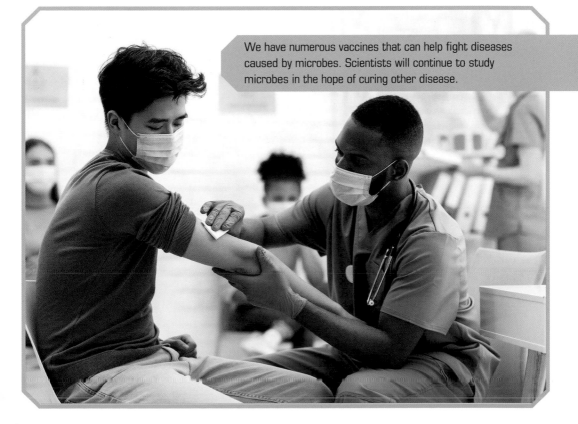

We have numerous vaccines that can help fight diseases caused by microbes. Scientists will continue to study microbes in the hope of curing other disease.

GLOSSARY

ANTIBIOTICS Substances produced by some microbes and fungi that kill other microbes or slow their growth. They are especially useful in treating infections caused by bacteria but not viruses.

CHROMOSOME A structure, containing genes, that is passed from parent to offspring.

DECOMPOSERS Organisms that break down dead organisms and recycle nutrients.

DIGESTION The process of breaking down food into simpler chemical compounds that can be absorbed and used by an organism.

DOMAIN The highest rank of organisms, higher than a kingdom.

ELECTRONS Tiny, negatively charged particles that orbit the positively charged nucleus of an atom.

ENZYMES Complex proteins that regulate the rates of biochemical reactions in an organism.

EPIDEMICS Outbreaks of diseases that affect a large number of people in an area at the same time.

ETIOLOGY Having to do with the cause of a disease.

EUKARYOTE Any organism with one or more cells that have visible nuclei and organelles.

FILAMENTS Very long, thin, cylindrical cells.

GENOME All the genetic information in an organism.

HEREDITY Transmission of information from one generation to the next through genes.

IMMUNE Having a high degree of resistance to a disease.

MEMBRANE A thin, flexible layer that allows some things, but not others, to pass through.

METHANE A colorless, odorless, flammable gas resulting from the decomposition of organic matter; it is also produced by some archaea.

MICROMETERS (MICRONS) Units of measure equal to one-millionth of a meter. A micrometer equals 0.000039 inch.

MUTATION A random change in a gene or chromosome that results in a new trait that can be inherited.

NUTRIENTS Matter organisms need to live and grow.

PARASITES Organisms that live in association with other organisms, obtaining advantages from the other organisms while usually harming them.

PH Measure of how acidic or basic a solution is. Values below 7 are acidic; values above 7 are basic.

PHOTOSYNTHESIS The process by which plants and some microbes produce food using air, sunlight, and water.

PROKARYOTE An organism whose DNA is not contained within a nucleus; for example, a bacterium.

PUS Thick, yellowish white fluid formed by the body in reaction to infection.

RECEPTORS Protein molecules that recognize and bind specific small molecules such as hormones.

SEPSIS An extreme bacterial infection in the body that can result in tissue damage, organ failure, and death.

SILICA A chemical compound composed of silicon and oxygen; it is the principal component of glass.

STERILIZE To free from living microbes, typically by heating.

TRANSMISSION ELECTRON MICROGRAPH A technology that uses a beam of electrons to capture an image of microscopic objects.

FOR MORE INFORMATION

AMERICAN SOCIETY FOR MICROBIOLOGY (ASM)

1752 N Street NW
Washington, DC 20036-2904
(202) 737-3600
Website: www.asm.org
The society's mission is to advance microbiology as a way to understand life processes and to apply and communicate this knowledge worldwide for the improvement of health and for environmental and economic well-being.

AMERICAN SOCIETY FOR VIROLOGY (ASV)

c/o Katherine R. Spindler
University of Michigan Medical School
Department of Medical Microbiology and Immunology
Health Science Campus
1150 West Medical Center Drive, 5635 Med
Sci II
Ann Arbor, MI 48109-5620
(734) 764-9686
Website: asv.org
The ASV provides a forum for investigators of human, animal, insect, plant, fungal, and bacterial viruses. The society's aim is to promote the exchange of information and stimulate discussion and collaboration among scientists active in all aspects of virology.

ASSOCIATION OF MEDICAL MICROBIOLOGY AND INFECTIOUS DISEASE CANADA (AMMI)

192 Bank Street
Ottawa, ON K2P 1W8
Canada
(613) 260-3233
Website: www.ammi.ca
The association's mission is to contribute to the health of people at risk of, or affected by, infectious diseases; support research and education in infectious diseases and medical microbiology; and develop guidelines and policies for the prevention, diagnosis, and management of infectious diseases.

CENTERS FOR DISEASE CONTROL AND PREVENTION
Office of Public Health Genomics
1600 Clifton Road
Atlanta, GA 30333
(800) 232-4636
Website: www.cdc.gov/genomics/
The Office of Public Health Genomics was founded in 1997 to help incorporate genomics into public health research, policy, and programs.

GENETICS SOCIETY OF AMERICA
6120 Executive Boulevard
Suite 550
Rockville, MD 20852
(240) 880-2000
Website: www.genetics-gsa.org
The GSA works to improve communication between geneticists, promote research, foster the training of the next generation of geneticists, and educate the public and government about advances in genetics and their consequences to individuals and society.

GENOME CANADA
150 Metcalfe Street, Suite 2100
Ottawa, ON K2P 1P1
Canada
(613) 751-4460
Website: www.genomecanada.ca/
Genome Canada is an organization dedicated to funding and managing genetic research projects.

MICROSCOPY SOCIETY OF AMERICA (MSA)
11130 Sunrise Valley Drive
Suite 350
Reston, VA 20190
(703) 234-4115
Website: www.microscopy.org
Founded in 1942, the MSA is dedicated to the promotion and advancement of techniques and applications of microscopy and microanalysis in all relevant scientific disciplines.

FOR FURTHER READING

Arney, Kat. *Exploring the Human Genome.* New York, NY: Rosen Publlishing, 2019.

Bainbridge, David. *How Zoologists Organize Things: The Art of Classification.* White Lion Publishing, 2020.

Bozzone, Donna M. *Understanding Microbes.* New York, NY: Enslow Publishing, 2018.

Eaton, Louise, and Kara Rogers (eds.). *Examining Fungi and Protists.* New York, NY: Rosen Education Service, 2018.

Hirsch, Rebecca E. *The Human Microbiome: The Germs That Keep You Healthy.* Breckenridge, CO: Twenty-First Century Books, 2016.

Hodgkins, Fran. *Finding a Covid-19 Vaccine.* San Diego, CA: Brightpoint Press, 2021.

Lew, Kristi. *Taxonomy: The Classification of Biological Organisms.* New York, NY: Enslow Publishing, 2018.

Merchant, Raina G., and Lesli J. Favor PhD. *How Eukaryotic and Prokaryotic Cells Differ.* New York, NY: Rosen Educational Service, 2015.

Moon, Walt K. *The COVID-19 Virus.* San Diego, CA: Brightpoint Press, 2021.

Robinson, Tara Rodden. *Genetics for Dummies (third edition).* Hoboken, NJ: John Wiley & Sons, 2020.

Stearns, Jennifer, Michael Surrette, and Julienne C. Kaiser. *Microbiology for Dummies.* Hoboken, NJ: John Wiley & Sons, 2019.

Stuart, Whitney, and Hans C. Andersson, MD. *Genomics: A Revolution in Health and Disease Discovery.* Minneapolis, MN: Twenty-First Century Books, 2021.

INDEX

PHOTO CREDITS